# HISTORY FROM OBJECTS

KU-222-636

# The vikings

**John Malam**

WAYLAND

Published in 2012 by Wayland
Copyright © Wayland 2012

Wayland, 338 Euston Road, London NW1 3BH
Wayland, Level 17/207 Kent Street, Sydney, NSW 2000

All rights reserved.

**British Library Cataloguing in Publication Data**
Malam, John, 1957–
The Vikings. — (History from objects)
1. Civilization, Viking—Juvenile literature. 2. Material
culture—Scandinavia—History—Juvenile literature.
I. Title II. Series
948'.022-dc22

ISBN: 978 0 7502 6766 3

Produced for Wayland by Calcium
Design: Paul Myerscough
Editor: Sarah Eason
Editor for Wayland: Camilla Lloyd
Illustrations: Geoff Ward
Picture research: Maria Joannou
Consultant: John Malam

4 6 8 10 9 7 5 3

Printed in China

**Pic credits**: Alamy Images: Interfoto 25t, Interfoto/Fine Arts 17b; Corbis: The Art Archive 13b, Ted Spiegel 13t,
Werner Forman 17t, 23b; Getty Images: Dorling Kindersley/Liz McAulay 12; Rex Features: Richard Gardner
18, Nils Jorgensen 8; Shutterstock: Algol 14t, Andrew Barker 5, 16, 26t, Bluecrayola 11t, 27b, JackF 11b, 26c,
Roman Kaplanski 3, 14b, Andrei Nekrassov 22, 26b, Tyler Olson 20, Photo25th 7, 27t, Igor Plotnikov 6, Anna
Stasevska 23t, Dusan Zidar 19; Topham Picturepoint: Firth 10; Wayland Picture Library: 21b, 24; Wikimedia
Commons: 15, Andrew Dunn 25b, Hedning 4, 21t, Thomas Ormston 9.

Cover photograph: Shutterstock/Photo25th

Wayland is a division of Hachette Children's Books, an Hachette UK company.

www.hachette.co.uk

| EAST RIDING OF YORKSHIRE SLS | |
|---|---|
| 901650981 | |
| Bertrams | 08/03/2014 |
| 948 | £8.99 |
| | |

# Contents

# Who were the Vikings?

The Vikings came from Scandinavia. This is an area in north-east Europe where Norway, Sweden and Denmark are today. The Vikings **conquered** and **settled** new lands for about 300 years, from AD 800 to 1100. This is called the Viking Age.

## The Viking world

The Vikings were great travellers. They explored Europe, North Africa, the Middle East, and the islands of the north Atlantic Ocean. Shetland, the Faroe Islands, Iceland and Greenland were stepping stones for their journeys, taking them further west. Eventually they crossed the Atlantic and reached Canada, becoming the first Europeans to set foot on North America.

 Norway and Sweden have mountains, forests and **fjords** (say fee-ords). Denmark does not have any mountains and is flat.

### SEA RAIDERS

The word Viking may come from the Scandinavian word 'viking', meaning pirate or sea-raider.

## Traders and raiders

On their travels, the Vikings came into contact with many different people. They were known as violent **warriors** but also as **traders**. As traders, Vikings sailed along rivers and across seas. They took jewels, walrus **ivory**, furs and **slaves**, which they traded for silver, gold, silk, spice, honey and wine. They raided **monasteries** and towns, stealing objects and taking prisoners.

## Settlers

Many Vikings moved away from their homeland. There was a shortage of farmland in Scandinavia, so they searched for new places to live. About 10,000 Vikings settled on Iceland, and 3,000 went to live on Greenland. Ireland, Britain, Russia and France also became their homes. Wherever they settled, they took the Viking way of life with them.

**Key**

Viking homelands

*Norway, Sweden and Denmark were the homelands of the Vikings.*

## What does it tell us?

Ships or boats were extremely important to Vikings. Longships carried warriors on raiding missions across Europe. Huge trading ships moved people, animals and **goods** over great distances.

# Towns and homes

There were no real towns in Scandinavia before the age of the Vikings. Instead, the landscape was dotted with farms and a few market-places. During the time of the Vikings, the first towns appeared.

## Trading goods

There were some market-places in Scandinavia. In these places, such as in Helgö in Sweden, large numbers of people gathered to trade goods. Market-places were used at certain times of the year. For a few days traders and craftspeople sold goods from **stalls** in the open air.

## First towns

At Ribe in Denmark, people stayed at the market all year round. By the early AD 800s it had become the first town in Scandinavia. Towns also developed in places where the Vikings settled, such as Dublin (Ireland), Novgorod (Russia) and York (England).

 *Town streets were busy, narrow places where rubbish was often left lying around.*

## What does it tell us?

This longhouse, at Stöng, Iceland, is a copy of a Viking longhouse. It has been made using the same materials the Vikings used. It shows us that the Vikings covered their roofs in thick turf to keep the house warm.

## Longhouses

In the countryside, Vikings lived in longhouses. They were farmhouses that looked like barns or halls. The family lived at one end and their farm animals at the other. In the middle was an open fire used for cooking and for keeping the house warm.

## Town houses

Town houses were smaller than longhouses. Most were single-storey buildings, usually made from wood, **wattle and daub** and **turf**. Some parts were used as workshops where craftsmen could make their goods.

### SMALL TOWN

All Viking towns were small compared to towns today. Even Hedeby, in Denmark, which was one of the largest towns, had fewer than 2,000 people.

# Farming and food

Most Vikings were farmers. They cleared forests or used rough land to make farms. On small farms the work was done by the farmer and his family. On larger farms, the Vikings used **slaves** to do the work.

## Crops

Cabbages, onions, beans and peas were the main vegetables grown. The main crops were cereals, especially oats, barley and rye. Oats were used to make porridge. Barley and rye were made into a **yeast**-free bread. It was too cold to grow wheat in many Viking lands, so wheat was brought in by traders.

## Food and drink

Meat came from pigs, sheep, goats and geese, and also from deer, horses, seals and whales. It was roasted, boiled, stewed or made into sausages, then served with vegetables. Vikings near the sea ate fish, shellfish and seabirds and their eggs. Butter and cheese came from milk, and honey was used to sweeten food. They drank milk, barley beer, and an alcoholic drink called **mead**, made from honey.

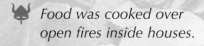 *Food was cooked over open fires inside houses.*

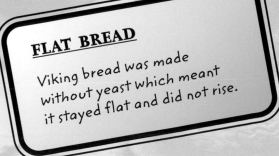

FLAT BREAD

Viking bread was made without yeast which meant it stayed flat and did not rise.

## Mealtimes

Vikings had two meals a day – the 'day meal', in the early morning, and the 'night meal', in the early evening. Food was cooked over the house fire, and was served in wooden bowls and on wooden plates called platters. They used metal knives and wooden or horn spoons, but did not have forks. Cups were made from wood, except in rich households where glass and silver ones were used.

 *The Vikings cooked their food in pots such as these, above.*

## What does it tell us?

Drinking horns like this were filled with beer or mead. They tell us that the Vikings enjoyed drinking. The horn could not be put down without spilling the contents – it had to be emptied in one go!

11

# clothes and crafts

Viking women made clothes for their families.
The poorer Vikings and slaves wore hard-wearing,
practical clothes that were not fashionable.
The clothes of richer Vikings were made
from more expensive materials.

## Viking clothes

Women wore ankle-length dresses, over which were
**tunics** held in place by shoulder brooches. Scarves
and caps covered their heads. Men wore knee-
length tunics and trousers, and leather or wool
caps. Both men and women wore flat leather
shoes or boots and woollen socks. In cold
weather they wrapped up in warm cloaks of
wool or fur. Children dressed as their parents
did, but girls kept their heads uncovered,
except in very cold weather.

## Clothes for the rich

Rich Vikings had clothes made from expensive silk
from China. Traders bought them at markets in the
east. The wealthy also had gold and silver threads
woven into patterns on their clothes.

### BAGGY TROUSERS

Vikings who met Arabs on their
travels copied their clothes, and
returned to Scandinavia wearing
loose-fitting baggy trousers.

 *A Viking
warrior would
have worn a
warm woollen
tunic, trousers
and tough,
leather boots.*

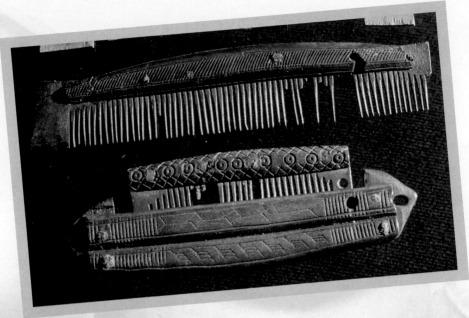

 *The teeth of Viking combs were close together to comb out knots and to catch head lice.*

## Viking crafts

The Vikings were skilled at many crafts, and they produced a wide range of everyday items. Pieces of animal bone and horn were made into combs, pins and spoons. Woodworkers made cups, bowls, platters, barrels for ale and furniture. Jewellers worked with **amber**, **jet** and glass to make beads and necklaces. They also made brooches, clasps and bracelets from **bronze** and silver.

## What does it tell us?

Brooches were always made of bronze metal. Rich women could have highly decorated brooches, which might also have been covered in a layer of gold.

13

# Ships and travel

The Vikings were great ship builders and travellers. They journeyed along rivers and sailed across wide seas. Several Viking ships have been found, which is how we know about them.

## Trade and transport ships

Viking ships were made from planks of wood, held together firmly with metal pins called rivets. A trader's ship was called a knarr. It was deep and wide with a big square sail. Its main job was to carry goods – although knarrs also carried people. Knarrs took settlers to new homes, and it was probably knarrs that were the first ships to sail from Europe to North America.

 A model of a Viking longship. These ships were used to transport bands of warriors.

## Warships for warriors

Viking warriors used longships. They are also known as dragonships, because a carving of a dragon was sometimes put at the prow (front). They had a sail, but most of the time they were rowed by the men on board. Longships were narrow and not too deep, so they could sail in shallow water and even come up on to beaches.

 The prow of a Viking longship, carved as a dragon.

## What does it tell us?

Sometimes important people were buried in ships. Two women's bodies were found in this ship. It was discovered at Oseberg in Norway and had been buried around AD 800.

## Crossing the seas

Viking sailors were also explorers. The Viking Leif Eriksson was a great explorer. In around AD 1000 he sailed west from Greenland in search of new land. After a few days he came to a land of rocks and **glaciers**. He then sailed south along the coast to a place with woods, rivers and wild grapes. He called it Vinland, which means Wine Land. We now know that he had reached the coast of Canada, North America.

### HEAVY LOAD

A knarr found at Hedeby, in Denmark, could carry a load weighing up to 38 tonnes — about the weight of six African elephants.

15

# Warriors and raiders

In AD 793, Vikings from Norway attacked Lindisfarne Island, off the north-east coast of England. It was the first Viking raid in history, and marked the start of raids across western Europe.

## Viking raids

Towns, villages and monasteries in Britain, Ireland and France were attacked by Vikings. They were searching for gold, silver and other valuable things. Gold and silver objects were cut into small pieces which could be easily carried and traded for goods, or melted down and made into new items. Prisoners were also taken and held for **ransom**. For example, the **abbot** of a French monastery was taken prisoner. He was only released after the French paid the Vikings an enormous amount of gold and silver.

Lindisfarne Island (also known as Holy Island). The Vikings attacked the monastery here in AD 793.

**SWORD NAMES**

Swords were valuable and were given names, such as Leggbítr (Leg-biter) and Fótbítr (Foot-biter).

# Warriors and weapons

The main Viking weapon was the sword. It had a long iron blade and was used to chop at an enemy, not to stab with the point. Other weapons included spears with iron tips, bows and arrows and heavy axes. A few warriors wore chain-mail armour made from tiny iron rings linked together. Warriors who couldn't afford chain mail wore leather jerkins (fitted jackets). Some wore iron helmets, but most made do with leather caps. Warriors carried round shields made from wood and leather.

 *An iron helmet with bronze decoration from Sweden. It has a guard to protect the wearer's nose.*

## What does it tell us?

This is the carving of a Viking 'beserker' warrior. It shows the warrior biting on his shield. The bravest Viking warriors were called 'beserkers'. Before battle they worked themselves into a rage – shouting and biting the edges of their shields. Our English expression 'to go beserk' comes from the name of these fighters.

# Sports and games

The Vikings found many ways to entertain themselves. They enjoyed playing games and sports as well as music and singing. At night they gathered round fires to listen to sagas and poems.

The Vikings played music with instruments such as musical horns, like the one shown below.

## Viking sports

In the summer, Vikings competed in foot races, swimming, wrestling and jumping. In the winter, they skated on frozen rivers and ponds, and skied across snow. Crowds watched horse racing and horse fighting. Owners would win money if their horse won.

For some games, such as throwing rocks, competitors had to be fit and strong. Warriors took part in archery contests, shooting arrows into the centre of a target. They also had sword fights. Both sports were good training for real fights and battles.

### HEAVY SWIMMING

It is said that in some Viking swimming competitions, the competitors wore their heavy armour to make it more difficult.

## Viking games

Board games played with counters and dice were very popular. The best known board game was hnefatafl ('king's table'), which was for two players. The winner was the first person to capture their opponent's king. It was a game that needed clever thinking – just like chess. Chess became a popular game towards the end of the Viking Age. It may have been learned by Vikings who had travelled to the east.

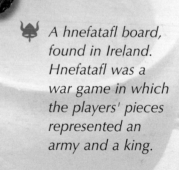

A hnefatafl board, found in Ireland. Hnefatafl was a war game in which the players' pieces represented an army and a king.

## What does it tell us?

This collection of Viking chess pieces was found on the Isle of Lewis, Scotland, in 1831. They had been carved in Norway from walrus ivory and whales' teeth. It shows us that some Vikings enjoyed playing chess.

# Quiz

1. **When was the Viking Age?**
   a. AD 600 to AD 900
   b. AD 800 to AD 1100
   c. AD 1200 to AD 1500

2. **Who lived inside a longhouse?**
   a. People only
   b. Farm animals only
   c. People and farm animals

3. **How many meals a day did Vikings have?**
   a. 1
   b. 2
   c. 3

4. **Which country did silk come from?**
   a. China
   b. Japan
   c. Russia

5. **Where was Vinland?**
   a. Canada
   b. Greenland
   c. Iceland

**6. What were the bravest Viking warriors called?**
   a. Raiders
   b. Skirmishers
   c. Berserkers

**7. What was a dowry?**
   a. A celebration meal
   b. A type of coat
   c. A gift of money, goods or property

**8. Who was king of the Viking gods?**
   a. Odin
   b. Thor
   c. Frey

**9. What were individual Viking letters called?**
   a. Skalds
   b. Runes
   c. Futhark

**10. The game of hnefatafl ('king's table') was played by how many players?**
   a. 2
   b. 4
   c. 6

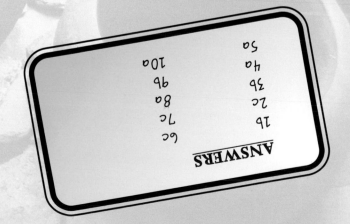

ANSWERS
6c
7c  8a  9b  10a
1b  2c  3b  4a  5a

# Timeline

| | |
|---|---|
| AD 793 | The first Viking raid in history, against a monastery on Lindisfarne, England. |
| c. AD 825 | The first Viking coins are minted. |
| AD 834–837 | Viking raids against towns in Germany, along the River Rhine. |
| c. AD 800 | A Viking longship is buried under a mound at Oseberg, Norway. |
| AD 839 | Vikings travel to Russia. |
| AD 841 | Viking settlers establish a base at Dublin, Ireland. |
| AD 845 | Vikings attack Paris, France, and Hamburg, Germany. |
| AD 860 | Vikings attack Constantinople (Istanbul), Turkey. |
| c. AD 860 | Vikings explore the coast of Iceland. |
| AD 862 | Viking settlers establish a base at Novgorod, Russia. |
| AD 865 | An army of Vikings from Denmark invades England. |
| AD 866 | Vikings capture York, and it becomes their main town in England. |
| c. AD 870s | Vikings begin to settle in Iceland. |
| AD 876–879 | Vikings begin to settle in eastern England. |
| AD 886 | England is divided in half – the north belongs to the Vikings, the south to the English. |
| AD 902 | The Vikings are thrown out of Dublin, Ireland. |
| c. AD 905 | A Viking longship is buried under a mound at Gokstad, Norway. |
| AD 912 | Vikings begin to settle in northern France. |
| c. AD 965 | Viking trade with the Middle East starts to slow down. |
| c. AD 985 | Vikings begin to settle on Greenland, led by Erik the Red. |
| AD 991 | The Vikings force the English to pay ransom money to stop attacks on England. |
| AD 995 | Olaf Tryggvason becomes king of Norway and sets about converting the Vikings to Christianity. |
| c. AD 1000 | Leif Eriksson, son of Erik the Red, explores the east coast of North America. |
| c. AD 1010 | Viking explorer Thorfinn Karlsefni attempts to build a settlement in North America. |
| c. AD 1015 | Vikings abandon their settlement in North America. |
| AD 1066 | A Viking army is defeated in England, at the Battle of Stamford Bridge. |
| AD 1100 | The Viking Age ends. |

# Glossary

**abbot** The head monk in a monastery, who is in charge of other monks.

**afterlife** A life believed to go on in a new place, after death in this world.

**amber** The fossilised resin from ancient trees, which is used to make jewellery.

**bronze** A yellowish metal mixed from copper and tin.

**conquer** To win people and land by using violence.

**fjord** A deep trench of water that runs inland from the sea.

**glacier** A mass of ice that moves slowly along a valley.

**goods** Things that are bought and sold.

**ivory** A tough white material that makes up an elephant's tusks.

**jet** A black-coloured precious stone.

**mead** An alcoholic drink made from honey and water.

**monastery** The building where monks live.

**myth** A well-known story which has been told for generations.

**pagan** A person who is not a Christian.

**ransom** Money paid to free a prisoner.

**sacrifice** Something done or given to make something happen, or please a god.

**saga** A long and detailed story or poem of Viking adventures.

**settle** To move into somewhere new and set up home.

**slave** A person who is someone else's property.

**stall** A table outside, which holds goods to be sold.

**spin** To twist bits of cotton or wool into thread.

**trader** Someone who buys and sells goods.

**tunic** A piece of clothing a little like a dress, with a hole for the head and arms.

**turf** A layer of grass with roots and soil.

**warrior** A man who fights for his country, people or money.

**wattle and daub** Inter-woven twigs and poles covered with a thick layer of clay, straw and manure.

**weave** To make fabric by crossing over strips of thread.

**yeast** A living substance that makes bread rise.

# Index

# History From Objects

**Contents of titles in the series:**

## The Egyptians
### 978 0 7502 6763 2

Who were the Egyptians?
Homes and towns
Farming and food
Clothes and crafts
Pharaohs
Pyramids and other tombs
Gods and temples
Mummies
The Egyptians at war
Writing
Quiz
Timeline

## The Romans
### 978 0 7502 6762 5

Who were the Romans?
City of Rome
Roman town houses
The countryside
Food and drink
Clothes and crafts
Children and schools
Romans and religion
Defending Rome
Entertainment
Quiz
Timeline

## The Victorians
### 978 0 7502 6764 9

Who were the Victorians?
The Industrial Revolution
Transport
The growth of cities
Houses and homes
Inventions and discoveries
Fashion and culture
Victorian families
Children - school or work?
Entertainment
Quiz
Timeline

## The Greeks
### 978 0 7502 6767 0

Who were the Greeks?
City of Athens
Greek town houses
Farming and food
Clothes and crafts
Writing and myths
Children and schools
Gods and temples
The Greeks at war
Entertainment
Quiz
Timeline

## The Tudors
### 978 0 7502 6765 6

Who were the Tudors?
The Tudors and religion
Tudor homes
Food and drink
Clothes
Children and schools
Castles and weapons
Ships and the navy
Royal splendour
Entertainment
Quiz
Timeline

## The Vikings
### 978 0 7502 6766 3

Who were the Vikings?
Towns and homes
Farming and food
Clothes and crafts
Ships and travel
Warriors and raiders
Families and children
Gods and religion
Writing and sagas
Sports and games
Quiz
Timeline

WAYLAND